THE ROYAL INSTITUTE OF PAINTERS IN WATER COLOURS

EDITED BY CHARLES HOLME

OFFICES OF ‚THE STUDIO,’ LONDON
PARIS, AND NEW YORK   MCMVI

PREFATORY NOTE

IN accordance with the course pursued in the preparation of the special number of THE STUDIO dealing with the "Old" Water-Colour Society, the Editor has confined the illustrations in the present volume to reproductions in colours of the original drawings. This has, naturally, limited the number of plates, and the work of many well-known painters could not, in consequence, be represented. But he believes that the selection he has made will be found to be representative of the varied phases of the art of water-colour painting as practised by past and present members of the Royal Institute.

To those who have kindly assisted him by the loan of original drawings the Editor tenders his cordial thanks, and in particular desires to acknowledge the aid he has in this way received from Mrs. Boughton; Dr. Dyce Brown; Mr. R. J. Coleman; Mr. Frankland Gaskell; Mrs. Gulich; Mr. Herman Hart; Mr. Alfred S. Henry; Mr. J. Henry Hill; Mr. A. T. Hollingsworth; The Rev. William MacGregor; Mr. Alexander M. Phillips; Mr. Cecil L. Phillips; Mr. Lawrence B. Phillips; Sir Cuthbert Quilter, Bart.; Mr. T. R. Way; and Messrs. Ernest Brown and Phillips.

He desires especially to acknowledge the courtesy of the President and Council of the Institute for allowing the reproduction of two diploma works.

LIST OF REPRODUCTIONS IN COLOUR

LIST OF REPRODUCTIONS IN COLOUR

A CHRONOLOGICAL LIST OF THE MEMBERS AND ASSOCIATES OF THE ROYAL INSTITUTE OF PAINTERS IN WATER COLOURS FROM THE FOUNDATION OF THE SOCIETY IN 1831 TO THE PRESENT TIME

N.B.—The names of those whose work is reproduced in the following pages are printed in capital letters)

MEM.

Foundation Members, 1831–2.

Joseph Powell
    (*President*, 1832)
William Cowen
James Fuge
Thomas Maisey
    (*President*, 1833)
Giles Firman Phillips
George Sidney Shepherd
William B. Sarsfield Taylor
Thomas Charles Wageman

1833   W. H. Bach
1833   J. M. Burbank
1833   Robert William Buss
1833   George Chambers
1833   Alfred Clint
1833   Thomas Sidney Cooper, R.A.
1833   Edward Duncan
1833   William Henry Kearney
1833   Thomas Lindsay
1833   M. Macpherson
1833   Ambrose Martin
1833   H. John Noblett
1833   E. J. Pasquier
1833   George Scharf
1833   Thomas Wood
1834   Valentine Bartholomew
1834   Gordon Bradley
1834   John Burgess, jun.
1834   J. A. Cahusac, F.R.S., F.S.A.
1834   George B. Campion

MEM.

1834   John Chase
1834   H. E. Downing
1834   Thomas Dunage
1834   James Fahey
1834   Rev. T. A. C. Firminger
1834   Benjamin Richard Green
1834   William N. Hardwick
1834   George Howse
1834   William Hudson
1834   George Henry Laporte
1834   William Oliver
1834   Henry Parsons Rivière
1834   Charles Harvey Weigall
1835   Mrs. Chase (Miss Mary Anne Rix)
1835   Louis Haghe
    (*Pres.*, 1873, *Hon. Pres.*, 1884)
1835   Mrs. Mary Harrison
1835   Miss Mary Anne Laporte
1835   François Rochard
1835   G. Sims
1835   Henry Warren
    (*Pres.*, 1839. *Hon. Pres.*, 1873)
1836   John Martin
1836   Douglas Morison
1836   John Edward Newton
1836   R. Kyrke Penson, F.S.A.
1836   William Robertson
1836   J. M. Tayler
1837   Miss Louisa Corbaux

CHRONOLOGICAL LIST OF MEMBERS AND ASSOCIATES

MEM.

MEM.		
1837		John Gilbert
1837		Lilburne Hicks
1837		Thomas Kearnan
1837		Edward Henry Wehnert
1838		Aaron Edwin Penley
1838		John Skinner Prout
1838		John Absolon
1838		Edward Henry Corbould
1838		Henry Johnston
1839		Henry Bright
1839		Miss Fanny Corbaux
1839		Thomas Sewell Robins
1839		Alfred Henry Taylor
1839		William Telbin

*ASSOC. MEM.

ASSOC.	MEM.	
1840	1841	Thomas Shotter Boys
1840	1848	F. J. D'Egville
1840	—	Sir Oswald Walter Brierley
1840	1841	William Knight Keeling
1840	—	Thomas Miles Richardson, sen.
1841	1845	David Cox, jun.
1841	1848	Henry Maplestone
1841	—	John M. Youngman
—	1841	Miss Sarah Setchel
1842	—	John Wykeham Archer
—	1842	Mrs. Mary Margetts
1842	1844	George Haydock Dodgson
1842	1843	Joseph John Jenkins
1842	1843	Francis William Topham
1843	—	Henry Jutsum
1845	1848	John Callow
1845	—	Miss Jane Sophia Egerton
1845	1848	William Lee
1846	1852	William Collingwood
1846	1861	Henry Clark Pidgeon
1846	1850	Charles Vacher
—	1846	Mrs. Harris (Miss Fanny Rosenberg)
—	1846	Miss Fanny Steers
1847	1849	Charles Davidson
1847	1848	John Henry Mole (*Vice-President*, 1884)

ASSOC.	MEM.	
1847	—	Henry Theobald
1848	1849	William Bennett
1848	1850	Robert Carrick
1848	—	Michael Angelo Hayes
1848	1850	David Hall McKewan
1848	1851	Thos. Leeson Rowbotham
1849	1854	Samuel Cook
—	1849	Mrs. William Oliver (Miss Emma Eburne)
1849	1851	Harrison Weir
1849	—	William Wyld
1850	—	Thomas Hartley Cromek
1852	1865	Augustus Jules Bouvier
1852	1856	Edmund George Warren
1854	—	Charles Brocky
—	1854	Miss Emily Farmer
1854	1879	Philip Mitchell
1854	1857	Josiah Wood Whymper
1856	1863	James George Philp
1857	—	Thomas Sutcliffe
1858	—	Edward Morin
1858	—	Gustave A. Simonau
1858	1859	Henry F. Tidey
1859	—	Joseph Middleton Jopling
1859	—	Edward Richardson
1860	1863	Edwin Hayes, R.H.A.
1860	1860	Carl Werner
—	1861	Mrs. William Duffield (Miss Mary Anne Rosenberg)
—	1861	Mrs. Henry Murray (Miss Elizabeth Heaphy)
1861	1866	Joseph Charles Reede
1862	1867	William Wood Deane
1862	1862	William Leighton Leitch
1863	1870	Charles Cattermole
1863	1864	HENRY GEO. HINE (*Vice-President*, 1887)
1863	1864	George Shalders
1864	1867	CHARLES GREEN
1864	—	William Lucas
1864	1875	William Luson Thomas
1865	1868	GUIDO R. BACH
—	1866	Mme. Rosa Bonheur (Honorary)

* Associates were only elected between 1840 and 1878.

CHRONOLOGICAL LIST OF MEMBERS AND ASSOCIATES

ASSOC.	MEM.		ASSOC.	MEM.	
—	1866	Louis Gallait (Honorary)	1874	1879	John Adam Houston, R.S.A.
1866	1868	George G. Kilburne	1874	—	John Wright Oakes, A.R.A.
—	1866	Jean Baptiste Madou (Honorary)	1874	1879	William Simpson
1866	1867	John Mogford	1874	1875	John Syer
1866	1879	John Sherrin	1874	1874	SIR JOHN TENNIEL
1866	1871	Lewis John Wood	—	1874	Miss Elizabeth Thompson (Lady Butler)
1867	1871	Richard Beavis	1874	1874	Joseph Wolf
—	1867	Mme. Henriette Browne (*née* de Saux) (Honorary)	—	1875	Mrs. John Angell (Miss Helen Cordelia Coleman)
—	1867	Frederick Goodall, R.A. (Honorary)	1875	1879	Miss Marion Chase
1867	1871	Edward Hargitt	—	1875	Miss Mary Gow
—	1867	John Rogers Herbert, R.A. (Honorary)	1875	1879	H. Towneley Green
1867	—	James Thompson Hixon	1875	1879	CHARLES EDWARD HOLLOWAY
1867	1870	SIR JAMES DROM-GOLE LINTON (*Vice-President*, 1883, *President*, 1884)	1875	1879	Charles Joseph Staniland
			1876	1879	JAMES AUMONIER
			1876	1879	Edwin Bale
—	1867	Daniel Maclise, R.A. (Honorary)	1876	1879	George Clausen, A.R.A.
1867	—	James Mahony	1876	1877	Seymour Lucas, R.A.
—	1867	J. L. Meissonier (Honorary)	—	1876	E. M. Ward, R.A. (Honorary)
—	1867	Sir John Everett Millais, Bart., P.R.A. (Honorary)	1877	1879	Thomas Walter Wilson
1867	1870	Henry Benjamin Roberts	1878	1879	JOHN FULLEYLOVE
1868	—	Valentine Walter Bromley	1878	1879	Harry Hine
1868	1870	Andrew Carrick Gow, R.A.	1878	1878	P. Falconer Poole, R.A.
1868	1870	Harry John Johnson		1879	G. H. BOUGHTON, R.A.
1870	1872	TOM COLLIER		1879	Lady Lindsay (of Balcarres
1870	1876	Edward Henry Fahey		1879	Sir Coutts Lindsay, Bart.
1870	1874	William Small		1879	Henry J. Stock
1871	1875	Hugh Carter		1879	Frank Wm. Warwick Topham
1871	1876	EDWARD JOHN GREGORY, R.A. (*President*, 1898)	1880		H. I. H. The Empress Frederick of Germany (Honorary)
1871	1873	Hubert Herkomer, R.A.	1880		Lionel P. Smythe, A.R.A.
1871	1873	Walter William May	1881		Mark Fisher
1871	1875	JAMES ORROCK	1882		H.R.H. Princess Henry of Battenberg (Honorary)
1871	1876	Frederick John Skill	1882		Charles Reginald Aston
—	1872	Joseph Israels (Honorary)	1882		RANDOLPH CALDE-COTT
1873	1875	EDMUND MORISON WIMPERIS (*Vice-President*, 1895)	1882		FREDERICK GEORGE COTMAN
1874	1877	James Hardy			

MEM.
1882 Walter Crane
1882 FRANK DILLON
1882 Charles Earle
1882 GEORGE S. ELGOOD
1882 KEELEY HALSWELLE, A.R.S.A.
1882 Dr. Edward Hamilton (Honorary)
1882 Colin Hunter, A.R.A.
1882 Charles Edward Johnson
1882 Joseph Knight
1882 Charles James Lewis
1882 Robert Walker Macbeth, R.A.
1882 Percy Macquoid
1882 Thomas R. Macquoid
1882 John Thomas Hamilton Macallum
1882 John MacWhirter, R.A.
1882 Alfred Parsons, A.R.A.
1882 Henry Pilleau
1882 John Isaac Richardson
1882 Arthur Severn
1882 Arthur Stocks
1882 Spencer Vincent (Honorary)
1882 FRANK WALTON
1882 John William Waterhouse, R.A.
1882 John White
1882 Richard Caton Woodville
1882 Wm. Lionel Wyllie, A.R.A.
1883 Edwin Austin Abbey, R.A.
1883 Thomas Huson
1883 WALTER LANGLEY
1883 Ludwig Passini
1883 J. R. Spencer Stanhope
1883 GEORGE FAULKNER WETHERBEE
1884 H.S.H. Count Gleichen (Honorary)
1884 FRANK DADD
1884 Charles Napier Hemy, A.R.A.
1884 Henry R. Steer
1885 Hector Caffieri
1885 Edward Combes, C.M.G. (Honorary)

MEM.
1885 Thomas Pyne
1885 John Scott
1885 Wm. Harris Weatherhead
1886 H.S.H. Prince Louis of Battenberg (Honorary)
1886 H. E. Count Seckendorff (Honorary)
1886 John Charles Dollman
1886 CLAUDE HAYES
1886 Mme. Térésa Hegg de Landerset
1886 Joseph Nash
1887 ALFRED EAST, A.R.A.
1887 Cyrus Johnson
1887 YEEND KING (*Vice-President*, 1901)
1887 Mrs. Lewis (Miss Jane M. Dealy)
1887 John O'Connor
1887 AUGUSTUS WALFORD WEEDON
1887 Miss Annie M. Youngman
1888 T. Austen Brown
1888 BERNARD WALTER EVANS
1888 Sir James C. Harris, K.C.V.O. (Honorary)
1888 William Hatherell
1888 Miss Alice Mary Hobson
1888 JULES LESSORE
1888 Miss Alice Squire
1888 William Barnes Wollen
1889 MISS KATE GREENAWAY
1889 Joshua Anderson Hague
1889 Carlton Alfred Smith
1889 Miss Kate Mary Whitley
1891 Edgar Bundy
1891 ROBERT FOWLER
1891 Max Ludby
1891 William Rainey
1892 Charles MacIver Grierson
1892 ST. GEORGE HARE
1892 George Sheridan Knowles
1892 ROBERT BUCHAN NISBET, R.S.A.

X

CHRONOLOGICAL LIST OF MEMBERS AND ASSOCIATES

THE HISTORY OF THE ROYAL INSTITUTE OF PAINTERS IN WATER COLOURS

URING the period of nearly thirty years which intervened between the founding of the Royal Society of Painters in Water Colours and that of its chief rival, the association which is now known as the Royal Institute of Painters in Water Colours, the condition of affairs in the British art world had undergone some very considerable changes. The purpose of the first society was to unite the scattered forces of the young but promising water-colour school, and to give to painters who worked in the water-colour medium some special encouragement which would assist them in their efforts to develop the possibilities of the particular form of practice that they had chosen to follow. At first there had been no difficulty in adequately fulfilling this purpose, for the number of eminent water colourists who did not belong to other art associations like the Royal Academy was so limited that the majority of them could easily be included in the ranks of the " Old Society."

Indeed, one of the best evidences of the adequacy of the " Old Society " during the earlier years of the nineteenth century is provided by the failure of any other association started on the same lines, or with the same programme, to establish itself permanently. For something like a quarter of a century this institution was able practically to defy competition, and to strengthen itself year by year by drawing away from its rivals the few artists whose powers were distinguished enough to command any wide attention. Many of the famous names which were inscribed upon its roll of members at this time had figured in the list of supporters of one or other of the competing exhibitions, but the competition in no case continued for any long period and the ultimate gathering into the Society of the men who might have made efficient rivalry possible seemed to be an almost inevitable process.

But, naturally, this condition of dignified and matter-of-course superiority could not endure for ever. The exertions of the Society on behalf of water-colour painting were bound to have the effect of improving greatly the status of the art and of adding considerably to the number of the efficient practitioners who sought to attract the attention of the public. As the number increased the difficulty of including them all in one association grew greater, until at last it became impossible to cope with. The " Old Society " certainly continued to choose from the rapidly growing band of accomplished water-colourists those whom it considered to be worthiest of recognition, but it was unable by the very nature of its constitution to keep pace in its elections of new members with the demands for admission made by the outside artists. It was a close society with a limited membership, and it neither had, nor desired to have, the large gallery space necessary for the accommodation of a host of contributors. Exclusiveness, or rather the most careful selection, was an essential part of its policy, and from this policy it was not prepared to depart despite the change in the condition of affairs with which it had to deal.

That this exclusiveness should be the cause of some degree of antagonism between the Society and the outside artists who wished to be admitted to its privileges was only to be expected. Throughout the history of all art institutions this antagonism has existed ; it is active enough at the present time, and, judging by an extract from a newspaper quoted by Mr. J. L. Roget in his exhaustive " History of the Old Water-Colour Society," this particular institution was not exempt from the common fate. This extract is worth reproducing because there is in it a specific reference to the foundation of the Institute. " The monopoly of this institution," it runs, " by the paltry, mercenary workings of its members, has contributed mainly to its corruption and degradation. It is a farce, a notorious farce and falsehood, to suppose that Academies and Institutions professedly ' for the promotion of the best interests of the Fine Arts,' are anything, in fact, but monopolies for the promotion of the selfish interests of the few that constitute them. This institution, for instance, is exclusive in the narrowest degree, as if measured by the minds of the Directors, and proceeds entirely on the profitable principle of ' the fewer the better cheer.' No one out of the pale of the Society, however much his work may eclipse their own (and, perhaps, for that prudent principle alone), is permitted to exhibit here, and the consequence is that many draftsmen of the finest talent, but disdainful of the mere slip-slop character of water-colour painters, are refused the *entrée* ; while those within, lining the walls, as it has been known, with fifty pictures by a single artist, spoil the exhibition by a dull, tedious monotony ; and if

ii R I

they can be said to reign in this confined region, it is because they are one-eyed monarchs of the blind. We say not this in disparagement of the genius of several of them, but in reprobation of the contemptible system which excludes the delightful variety which might be produced by admitting a few of the sparkling productions of the more powerful masters. This illiberal policy, the offspring of sordid ignorance, has over-reached itself, and set afoot another gallery on a more enlightened and encouraging principle."

Despite the ridiculous exaggeration of this attack, with its revelation of personal animosity and stupid intolerance, it is significant because it shows how quickly the need had arisen for a widening of the opportunities open to painters in water colour. The " Old Society " had been in existence for only twenty-seven years when this bitter comment appeared—it was published in 1831—but already there was room for another association with the same mission. This was proved by the fact that the gallery, " on a more enlightened and encouraging principle," was able to commence then a career which has continued with much distinction to the present day. Its fate has been very unlike that of "The New Society of Painters in Water Colours," which was formed in 1807, changed its name to " The Associated Artists in Water Colours " in 1808, and succumbed under an accumulation of financial difficulties in 1812. The final experience of the artists who exhibited with this short-lived association was to see their works which were on view in the show held in that year seized and sold by the landlord of the gallery to pay arrears of rent. Evidently in 1812 the " Old Society " was quite able to meet what demand there was for the exhibition of water colours, and could gather under its roof practically all the men who had any real standing as workers in the medium. But less than twenty years later there was a new generation of workers to reckon with, and this altered condition led necessarily to fresh and more efficient competition. By then there had been so much progress in the development of our water colour school that competition neither weakened the " Old Society " nor destroyed the competitor, but instead gave to the water colourists a necessary increase of opportunities for setting their claims to attention before the people who were interested in the art.

So in 1831 a small band of artists combined to organise a society which was to make the encouragement of the non-privileged worker an essential part of its policy. They added a further complication to the history of water-colour painting by naming their association

" The New Society of Painters in Water Colours," and by opening, in 1832, their first exhibition in the same rooms, at 16, New Bond Street, which had been occupied by the defunct institution originally called by the same title. They still more complicated matters in 1833 when they altered their name to " The Associated Artists in Water Colours," wilfully, it would seem, continuing the parallel with their predecessor ; and in 1834 they reverted to their first title, and were known once more as the " New Society of Painters in Water Colours "—and the " New Society " they remained for thirty years. These confusing changes were signs of much dissension in the ranks of the association, of dissensions great enough to threaten its very existence, and to make very doubtful its chances of ultimate success. During its first few years, indeed, it experienced some serious vicissitudes which in all probability would have abruptly ended its career if it had not had so obviously a mission to fulfil ; and as a consequence considerable modifications were introduced into the working scheme which had been originally laid down.

One of the first ideas entertained by the promoters was that the exhibitions of the society should be open to all comers. This, in fact, was the " more enlightened and encouraging principle " which was to make the new venture so superior to the " Old Society," and to give it such special claims to attention as a disinterested opponent of privilege and monopoly. As a result of this policy, there were in the inaugural show, in 1832, as many as a hundred and twenty exhibitors, who contributed three hundred and thirty drawings, and in the following year the exhibitors had increased to a hundred and seventy. These shows met with a very large measure of success ; they attracted a satisfactory number of visitors, and the record of sales was decidedly good. So promising a beginning was doubtless due in some measure to the efforts made by the originators to advertise their undertaking ; they sent round circulars broadcast to all kinds of artists, and they took care to enlist as supporters certain influential amateurs and art lovers. But a very brief experience sufficed to prove that the policy and the system of management were not conducive to smooth working. Apparently the heads of some of the people responsible for the control of the Society were turned by the welcome accorded by the public, and as a consequence the dissensions already referred to speedily arose.

What was the nature of the trouble can be judged from an extract from a book, " Fine Arts in Great Britain and Ireland," written in 1841 by W. B. Sarsfield Taylor, one of the foundation members of the " New Society." In the brief summing up which he gives of

iv R I

the history of the Association he says : "But success, as we have seen in other cases, was the parent of cabal. Some of the members of inferior talent formed the project of getting the whole affair under their own control, and as that class composed the majority they succeeded in disgusting the respectable men, whose talents and respectability had established the exhibition. These gentlemen, of course, resigned. The cabal soon blundered into a lawsuit and various other foolish and extravagant contrivances during two or three years, until some better artists and more sensible men getting in amongst them, at a moment when the affair was nearly ruined, the new men turned out the leader of the cabal, a man named Maisey, who had usurped the office of President, and from that time their affairs seemed to have been going on very well." In this account there may be some colouring of personal feeling, for Sarsfield Taylor was one of the "respectable men" who resigned in disgust at the scheming of the "members of inferior talent," and no doubt memories of the fights between the two parties into which the Society was divided were, when he wrote, still rankling in his mind.

But certainly he did not exaggerate when he said that the affair was nearly ruined by the foolish and extravagant contrivances of the people who were more anxious to advance what they conceived to be their own interests than to work for the benefit of the association as a whole. Things, indeed, came to such a pass that in 1834 a great deal more had to be done, besides the turning out of the "man named Maisey" from the presidentship, to save the society from being hopelessly wrecked. A complete scheme of reconstruction was drawn up which involved the abandonment of much that had been included in the original programme. The most drastic alteration was the closing of the exhibitions to outside artists, a change which showed how little the idea of opposing the principle of the "Old Society" commended itself to the men who were most concerned with the establishing of the new body on a safe and workable basis. When the reconstituted society began operations in 1835 it had committed itself to more or less close imitation of its older competitor, and on these lines it continued to run for nearly fifty years.

This 1835 exhibition was not held in the Bond Street gallery which had been the scene of the previous three shows. The society, which then consisted of twenty-five members, made still more evident the break with its earlier associations by moving to a room at Exeter Hall, where it remained for three years ; and then, in 1838, it established itself at 38, Pall Mall. By that time it had settled down into quiet and satisfactory prosperity ; it had gained a recognised position, and was able to attract to its ranks many of the more distinguished among the younger artists who had not already been appropriated by its rival. Consequently its exhibitions secured a very fair share of popularity, and quickly came to be regarded as welcome additions to the comparatively limited number of shows which were at that period open to the inspection of the public. Even while the society was going through the painful process of being hammered into shape, and while it was suffering severely from the infantile disorders which are apt to trouble such complicated organisations, it had not failed to draw the attention of people who were interested in water-colour painting, so directly it was in proper working order it began to gather round it a band of supporters quite large enough to ensure the success of the undertaking.

It is by no means improbable that the admission of the amateur element into the society as it was at first constituted was one of the causes of the trouble which brought the concern, after its excellent beginning, to the verge of irreparable disaster. A certain incompatibility in point of view was bound sooner or later to separate the professional artists from the men associated with them who worked simply for amusement or to gratify a taste for art ; and out of this incompatibility would come inevitably a division of interests and the arraying of one party against another. This division of interests would naturally be encouraged by the fact that the exhibitions were open to all classes of contributors, because consideration would have to be given to the demands of the amateur even though they might be antagonistic to the desires of the professional artist. Such mixed societies have not often enjoyed any long spell of prosperity, and, though they have been frequently attempted, they have usually failed through lack of sufficient cohesion. Fortunately the " New Society " had in it a professional party strong enough to force on a sane and practical reconstruction, and to get rid of the most dangerous defects in the original constitution. Otherwise its history might have ended abruptly in 1834 when " the cabal blundered into a law-suit and various other foolish and extravagant contrivances."

One very perceptible result of this change in policy and methods was a definite improvement in the quality of the recruits whom the society was able to secure. From 1834 onwards the names inscribed upon the roll of members are those of painters who have now much more important places in art history than could be assigned to the

vi R I

majority of the earlier contributors. Sarsfield Taylor's assertion that prior to the reconstruction members of inferior talent composed the majority seems to have been justified, but the double processs of introducing " better artists and more sensible men," and of eliminating those of " inferior talent " had certainly a beneficial effect, and made possible a considerable raising of the standard set by the society. The steady growth in the popularity of the exhibitions held under the new constitution, and the better position taken by the society when it became a close body, were due, it can well be imagined, to the more convincing character of the works of art presented in its gallery. It began to meet the " Old Society " on more equal terms, and its rivalry with its more firmly established competitor no doubt helped to secure for it the attention and the sympathy of a large section of the public.

But by making this commendable effort to bring into its ranks only artists of recognised standing the " New Society " laid itself open to the risk of having many of its members carried away periodically by its rival. It became to some extent a stepping stone to the " Old Society," because a number of the water-colour painters whose merits it was the first to recognise were unable to resist the temptation to pass on into the other association, which seemed to them to offer superior advantages of seniority and professional position. That this tendency should have been developed is, of course, not surprising ; it is only in accordance with human nature that a man with a reputation to make, and profit by, should seek to turn to the fullest account what might be regarded as opportunities for advancement. But that repeated secessions of this character to some extent hindered the progress of the Institute is sufficiently obvious. Annually there were more gaps to be filled than would have been created by purely natural causes, and if the supply of capable men from without had not more than kept pace with the demands of both societies, the younger of the two might well have succumbed under such a continuous drain upon its resources. Fortunately the area of selection was widening year by year, and the additions to the band of candidates waiting for admission far outnumbered the vacancies caused by deaths and secessions.

Some of the disappearances, like that of the " respectable men " who dramatically shook from off their feet the dust raised by the unre-formed society during its first troublesome years, were direct consequences of internal squabbles. All causes of dispute were not removed by reconstruction, and even under the amended constitution there still remained subjects over which more or less serious differences of opinion were likely to arise. Differences of this sort brought about a kind of crisis some eight or nine years after the society had settled in Pall Mall, and several dissentient members withdrew. Among them were Edward Duncan, G. H. Dodgson, F. W. Topham, David Cox, Junr., John Callow, H. P. Rivière, and J. J. Jenkins, who all left between 1846 and 1850, and were received almost immediately into the " Old Society " ; and a year or two later the same convenient exchange was made by Charles Davidson and W. G. Collingwood. If all these withdrawals resulted from the condition of unrest which prevailed at the moment in the Pall Mall gallery, the junior society may well be said to have been once more on the verge of disaster, for it lost then a group of men who would have done much to establish it among the chief art institutions in this country—as can, indeed, be seen by the prominence of the parts they subsequently played in the affairs of the other institution by which they were welcomed.

However, the young society weathered this storm as it had those which had previously threatened it with shipwreck ; and though it suffered appreciably in the process it had vitality enough to enable it to go on with its work without interruption. If the places of the men who had gone overboard in the breeze could not be filled by artists of quite as commanding ability, there were always plenty of available recruits whose merits were sufficient to justify their election, so that the number of members was not allowed to fall seriously below its normal level. During this period candidates were required to pass through the preliminary stage of associateship before they could aspire to the full privileges of membership. This division of the society into two classes was started in 1840, and it continued until 1879, when a reversion was made to the original system, which has been maintained to the present day.

In 1858 an incident occurred which shows that the institution felt sure enough of itself to take the lead in an ambitious scheme for advancing the interests of the water-colour school as a whole. This scheme was set forth in a letter written by Henry Warren, the President of the " New Society," to Frederick Tayler, who was then at the head of the " Old Society." In this letter, which is quoted in Mr. Roget's history, reference is made to the rumoured intention of the Government to provide the Royal Academy with a site for an exhibition building, and a suggestion is advanced that the claims of the water-colour painters to consideration ought to be put forward in the event of any such grant being decided upon. The Academy was at that time in possession of rooms in the National Gallery building in Trafalgar Square, and as these rooms were required for the proper accommodation of the national collections, negotiations had been opened with a view of determining in what form it was to be compensated for its approaching ejection. The idea favoured by the Government officials was that the Academy should be assigned, on certain conditions, a piece of ground on which it could erect its own rooms ; and it was the probability that this idea would be adopted that induced Warren to invite the co-operation of the body over which Tayler presided.

The invitation was put in these words : "It has been hinted by influential parties to some of our members that the water-colour artists ought to participate in such grant, and we have considered the propriety of memorialising the Government. But it is thought that such memorial would be stronger if representing water-colour art generally, and that the two societies should either memorialise conjointly, or at any rate simultaneously." Tayler's answer was courteous but non-committal. He wrote, stating that in the view of the members of his society who were given an opportunity of expressing their opinion at the annual meeting in November, 1858, the matter was not far enough advanced to admit of any definite action being taken, but that he felt that there could be "but one opinion amongst water-colour painters as to the desirableness of securing for their branch of art its just and proper recognition." His letter left matters just where they were, and evidently it implied, without, however, any definite statement to that effect, that joint action was unlikely.

But some three months later the full intentions of the Government were revealed, and it became known that the ground occupied by Burlington House and its gardens was to be divided between the Royal Academy and a number of other institutions of an educational character. The "Old Society" at once appointed a committee of members to consider the position, and this committee came to the conclusion that their policy would be to take an independent course in applying to Parliament for a share in the available space. So both societies presented petitions to the House of Lords ; both were well supported, but in the end neither were successful. Whether the result would have been different if Warren's suggestion of a combined appeal had been adopted it is impossible to say ; but as a very rigorous selection had to be made from a multitude of applicants it is probable that the water-colour school would anyhow have been denied its "just and proper recognition." By satisfying the demands of the Academy the Government had

done all that it considered necessary for the encouragement
of art.

So the " New Society," disappointed in its desire to obtain official
support, or to induce its rival to take any steps in the direction of
amalgamation—an idea which may possibly have inspired Warren
in his suggestion for united action—set to work at once to build
a new gallery in Pall Mall not far from the rooms it had occupied
since 1838. The modest dimensions of this gallery seemed to imply
that the members had at the moment no idea of expansion or of
making any change in the conduct of their affairs. They had
apparently reverted to their original scheme of operations, and were
content to plod along in the way which, as their past experience
proved, was likely to lead them to solid prosperity. They were
clearly at peace with one another now, and there were no divergences
among them on questions of policy to interfere with their steady
progress as an art association.

They were, however, still quite ready to take part in any movement
which promised to affect the status of water-colour painting. For
example, in 1862 they were associated with the " Old Society " in
certain negotiations with the Commissioners of the London International Exhibition. The object of these negotiations was to safe-
guard the water colourists and to ensure a proper supervision for the
section of the exhibition which was to be devoted to works in this
medium. The Commissioners had drawn up a list of institutions
which they proposed to consult, and in this list both societies were
included. So the two Presidents, Warren and Tayler, addressed to
the Commissioners an enquiry, to which the signatures of both were
appended, as to the propositions of the exhibition authorities, and
asking that the control of the water-colour section should be
entrusted to delegates chosen from the two bodies. The reason
advanced for this request was that " the great bulk of the contributions will be made by artists who have been members of these
societies," a quite legitimate contention which certainly deserved
serious consideration.

But the Commissioners did not view the matter in the proper light.
As is usual on these occasions, the power was put into the hands of
members of the Academy, and Messrs. Redgrave and Creswick were
chosen to hang the works in oil and water colour which were to
appear in the exhibition. An answer to this effect was returned by
the Secretary of the Commission to the letter of the two Presidents ;
but, with the idea, perhaps, of making less evident what was really
a piece of official discourtesy, an offer was made to give to Warren

X R I

and Tayler passes which would allow them to enter the exhibition galleries while the hanging was in progress, when, as the Secretary put it, " I have no doubt that Mr. Redgrave will be glad to have the benefit of your advice and experience." This unfortunate offer was naturally resented by the Presidents, and they declined to accept the passes even when they were sent after Warren and Tayler had refused to be placed in such an impossible position.

Their answer to the communication of the Secretary of the Commissioners embodied a dignified and sensible protest against what was undeniably an injustice to water-colour painters and to the two associations which had done so much to give coherence to what had by this time become one of the greatest artistic developments which this country has seen. An extract from this protest can be quoted from Mr. Roget's book because it shows how correct was the position they took up : " We venture to state that the Department of Water Colour Art is not satisfactorily dealt with. In Paris, in 1855, the Presidents were invited to superintend the arrangements of these works. They are now in the hands of those who have no practical interest in this branch of art, and in whom, consequently, the water-colour painters fail to have confidence. We have had some experience in the anxiety and difficulty of arranging ordinary exhibitions, and we believe it to be out of the power of any two gentlemen to do justice to the claims of those artists who will confide their works to the International Exhibition. The Water Colour Societies were formed for the special purpose of advancing an art peculiarly British, and it seems reasonable that those most interested in its honour should have the opportunity of placing it before the world in the most advantageous manner." That the Societies had the best of the argument is decidedly not to be disputed, but unfortunately they had to be content with a moral victory. They gained nothing else by their display of public spirit.

It is by no means unlikely that the selection of two members of the Academy to deal with water colours in the exhibition was greatly responsible for the attitude taken up by Warren and Tayler. When they said that the arrangements had been put into " the hands of those who have no practical interest in this branch of art, and in whom, consequently, the water-colour painters fail to have confidence," they had probably in mind the traditional grievance which more than half a century before had spurred the water colourists to independent organisation. The Academy had never treated the art of water-colour painting as one which ought to be taken seriously ;

it had, indeed, rather gone out of its way to fix upon workers in the medium the stamp of inferiority, and to ticket them as unworthy to be counted among the leaders of the profession. Among its earliest rules was one which specifically disqualified painters in water colour only from admission to its ranks; and this rule had produced a distinctly bad effect, for it had induced many water colourists of high repute to abandon their own particular art for oil painting, so that they might become eligible for election into the Academy. No wonder that the Presidents of two societies of which the very existence signified a protest against Academic intolerance and neglect complained that the hangers at the International Exhibition had no practical interest in this branch of art, and were men in whom water colourists failed to feel confidence; and no wonder that they refused to accept in connection with the arrangement of the exhibition an advisory position which not only gave them no authority but even insisted upon their professional unimportance. If nothing but an incidental display of a few water colours in the art section of the International Exhibition had been intended the indifference of the Commissioners would not have mattered so much, but as what was finally brought together was a collection, chronologically arranged, of well over six hundred drawings, it is obvious that the assistance of two such experts as Warren and Tayler would have been invaluable. They might well have been supposed to know best what was the condition of the art at that period, and to be properly acquainted with the various stages of its history. Moreover, as the heads of two exclusively water-colour societies with a record, in the case of the older institution of nearly sixty years, and in the case of the junior of just over thirty, they were the people who should have been first consulted, if only as a matter of courtesy. The episode altogether is worth dwelling upon because it is throughout particularly significant. It shows what was the conventional attitude towards this " peculiarly British art," and it throws much light upon the difficulties which had to be overcome in the formation and organising of a school which has achieved high distinction through the number and ability of its members. The " New Society " ceased to be officially known by that name in 1863, and adopted instead the title of " The Institute of Painters in Water Colours." The change was certainly an improvement, for it put an end to the confusion which had been caused by the close resemblance between the designations of the two bodies, and it gave to the younger one a more definite standing. By calling itself " The Institute " the " New Society " ceased to advertise the fact that it was an association of comparatively recent creation and professedly in competition with a society which had naturally an advantage in a much longer record of successful working. In other respects it remained as it was before, making no alteration in its constitution and abandoning none of its aims to take and retain an honourable place among the institutions by which the progress of British art in its many phases is directed.

In this same year the first suggestion of an amalgamation of the old and new societies seems to have been put forward. It was nothing more than a suggestion, and it was never seriously considered, but it may be mentioned because there were apparently people even then who thought such an arrangement possible. It arose in connection with the Commission appointed to enquire into the position and responsibilities of the Royal Academy. This Commission went beyond what was professedly its purpose and attempted some kind of investigation of the affairs of other artistic associations. The "Old Society" was one of those which received attention, and its president, Tayler, was examined before the Commission. He declined, however, to give the information required, on the ground that a revelation of the private concerns of the society would be contrary to its interests and would put the public in possession of details which were better kept secret. But he wrote a letter to Lord Elcho, from whom seemingly had come alternative suggestions that the society should be absorbed by the Academy or that it and the Institute should amalgamate, opposing strongly both propositions. A junction with the Academy was, he pointed out, impossible as matters stood, and an alliance between the two water-colour societies was hardly more practicable because "the one would not be willing to admit its great inferiority to the other, and on equal terms a fusion could not fairly take place." The "Old Society," in fact, valued its independence and was in a condition of perfect stability, which justified the belief that it could continue to do its work in the world with all necessary efficiency ; and the Institute was playing very ably a by no means undistinguished second part. Its position was hardly one of "great inferiority," but as the junior institution it would, in any attempt at fusion, have had to sacrifice too much to make such an arrangement practicable.

A digression here is permissible to deal with the history of another organisation of water-colour painters which was destined to have somewhat close relations with both societies. It came into existence in 1865 and after supplying them year by year with a large number of new Associates was finally united with the Institute at the end of the year 1882. This organisation was known as "The General Exhibition of Water-Colour Drawings," and it established itself at the Egyptian Hall in the room called the Dudley Gallery, which has lately been demolished. Its intentions were set forth in a preface to the catalogue of the first exhibition : " the promoters of the exhibition, now for the first time opened, have had for their object the establishment of a gallery, which, while exclusively devoted to drawings as distinguished from oil paintings, should not in its use by exhibitors involve membership of a society. These two conditions are not at present fulfilled by any London exhibition. The water-colour societies reserve their walls entirely for members, while those galleries which are comparatively open to all exhibitors (such as that of the Royal Academy) afford but a limited and subordinate space to all works in other materials than oil. The exhibition is, therefore, not that of a new society, nor is it intended in any way to rival existing exhibitions. Its establishment has been called for solely by the requirements of very many artists—requirements of which the reality is evidenced by the large number of works sent in for exhibition. The promoters trust that the success of this their experiment may be such as to justify the hope they entertain of the exhibition becoming annual."

This expectation was certainly well founded : not only did the show become an annual affair, but for seventeen years it continued to receive efficient support from the best among the younger artists of the time. There was, in fact, a necessity for its existence ; history was repeating itself, and the position of affairs which had produced such definite results in 1831 was once more present. The number of artists of recognised and indisputable capacity had been steadily growing during this period of some thirty years, and there were in 1865 more able water colourists than the two close societies could accommodate without making considerable alterations in their rules for the admission of candidates. A place was wanted, too, where the younger men, who had not yet reached positions of such prominence that they could expect to be received by one society or the other at the first opportunity, could keep themselves properly before the public and make a really effective bid for the favour of their seniors in the profession. The " General Exhibition " provided just what was necessary—a show-room where artists could exhibit their work under conditions not too exacting, and with the knowledge that a reasonably high standard would be maintained in the collections periodically brought together.

The management of the " Dudley," as the " General Exhibition "

xiv R I

was soon called by everyone, was in the hands of a committee of artists and amateurs, and its financial position was secured at the outset by the formation of a large body of guarantors, who insured it against loss in the event of its income from the payments of visitors for admission, and from the commissions charged on sales, being insufficient to meet expenses. A short time after the water-colour exhibition was started two other annual shows were included in the scheme—one of cabinet pictures in oils, and another of black-and-white drawings and studies. All these shows achieved a very large measure of success; they were looked upon as institutions hardly less important than the exhibitions of the regularly constituted societies, and they never lacked support from the chief of the coming men. Indeed, a list of artists who made, or enhanced, their reputations by the aid of "The Dudley" would include a very large proportion of the names which are now given honourable places on the roll of the British school. The concern, unlike a formally constituted society, was not bound by more or less rigid traditions; it asked only that the contributors should show a proper degree of proficiency in their craft; and if this very necessary condition were observed, it was ready to recognise the widest variety of intention, and to admit the most diverse types of accomplishment.

Certainly it played a notable part in the history of both the water-colour societies by providing them with a succession of eminently suitable candidates, and by enabling them to fill up vacancies with men who were already well advanced in the popular favour. The "Old Society" drew very largely upon the stock of water-colour painters offered by "The Dudley," and the Institute also obtained from this source some of the best men who joined it during the seventeen years or so that intervened between the establishing of the "General Exhibition" and its own change of constitution in 1882. Among these men may be noted some like Richard Beavis, Walter Crane, and Hubert von Herkomer, who subsequently passed from the Institute to the "Old Society"; but most of the others remained faithful to the association which had been the first to welcome them into its ranks, and did their best to advance its interests. The creation of "The Dudley" may, indeed, be accounted a very fortunate circumstance, as it got rid of what is always a difficulty in the management of close societies—the proper estimation of the claims of candidates who come up for election. When artists are required to submit specimens of their work to a body of judges, and are expected, if they are unknown men, to stand or fall by the few examples that they are able to bring together for the occasion, they are exposed to a test that is always severe, and sometimes unfair. They may gain a favourable verdict because by happy accident they have been able to show the very pick of their performance, or they may be rejected because two or three isolated specimens of their practice are insufficient to illustrate their merits convincingly.

But when, year after year, practically all the coming water colourists could be seen in competition one with the other in a reputable exhibition, where the judges who were entrusted with the duty of making a right selection could watch the progress of promising youngsters without being obliged to wander in a perpetual pilgrimage from gallery to gallery, a much more correct appreciation of the relative importance of the men whom they were disposed to consider became immediately possible. It was easy, too, to see whether this or that candidate was likely to prove a desirable member and to keep up the standard of his performance when he had been called within the haven of privilege, or whether he had tendencies towards conventionality which would develop directly he ceased to be under the stress of competition. To the leaders of the " Old Society " and the Institute " The Dudley " shows must have been extremely interesting, and well worth studying ; they must have saved them many discussions when the claims of would-be Associates had to be put to the vote.

No gradual decay or waning of usefulness marked the last stages of " The Dudley " ; it ended by being absorbed into the Institute, which elected as members nearly all the men who were at the moment taking an active part in the management of the exhibitions. In 1882, when this arrangement was made, the Institute had just brought to conclusion the working out of a scheme which, after some years of preparation, promised to put it in a position of very great authority. This scheme was of an extremely ambitious nature, conceived on large lines, and in intention eminently sound. Circumstances prevented its complete realisation, but for this the members of the Institute cannot be blamed ; there was no lack of energy on their part, and they certainly did not fail to make the most of their opportunities of completing effectively the plan they had devised. They were unable, however, to unite all the forces which had to be allied before the undertaking could be carried out in its entirety, and they had accordingly to be satisfied with but a partial success.

Early in the seventies there had sprung up among the more

XVI R I

energetic and progressive men who had come into the Institute a feeling that its constitution was too inelastic and too narrow in scope to meet the demands of the ever-increasing body of artists whose interests they wished to consider. They feared that as a close society it was more likely to decrease than increase in influence, and that if it did nothing to bring itself up to date it would sooner or later fall out of the race, and cease to play any part in the affairs of the art world. No doubt they had learned a lesson from the prosperity of "The Dudley." There was an annual exhibition, open to all comers, which was enjoying in a marked degree the favour of the public. It was gathering to support it a band of prominent workers which, despite the drafts made upon it by the two societies, was steadily increasing in numbers, and threatening more and more to overshadow the formal institutions that were forbidden by their rules to take any liberal view of their responsibilities. Such a proof of the strength of the outside element seemed to the reformers within the Institute sufficient to justify them in planning a complete change of policy, and in seeking to enlarge enormously the scope of their activity.

But first of all they saw that they must alter the manner in which the internal affairs of the Institute were directed. The distinction between full Members and Associates, between the men who by virtue of their membership exercised sole control over the working of the concern, and the Associates who had the right to exhibit in the gallery, but were excluded from all participation in details of management, must be abolished. It had led to an objectionable narrowing down of the administration. The power was in the hands of only a few individuals, and those, too often, old men who were more anxious to maintain obsolete arrangements than to make an effort to move with the times. There was consequently a tendency towards stereotyped procedure, to a kind of fossilized system which kept the direction from being influenced by new ideas, and caused the society to lag every year more evidently behind its younger competitors.

So a proposition was put forward that the Associate class should be abolished. This was, of course, vehemently resisted by the older section, and the matter was debated with some bitterness on more than one occasion. At last it was formally brought up at a general meeting, and after a stormy discussion defeated for the moment by the votes of the men who believed in keeping things as they were. The advocates of reform were, however, not so easily to be turned from their purpose. They held an informal gathering immediately

afterwards, and drew up an ultimatum which threatened the resignation of the whole of the younger party if their demands were
not conceded. As such a secession would have meant practically
destruction, for it would have taken out of the Institute not only
the Associates, who naturally supported the new scheme, but also
a considerable proportion of the full Members, the upholders of
tradition had no alternative but to surrender with the best grace
they could muster. They saw that the opposition was determined
to have its way, and that if they held out any longer they would be
set the impossible task of keeping alive an association which had
suddenly been deprived of all its more active supporters. Accordingly
they withdrew their veto and consented to the change.

This was in 1879 ; by 1881 the scheme which had been so
vigorously inaugurated had taken a very definite shape. The
Members who were in favour of it, reinforced by a strong contingent
of promoted Associates, had a large majority, and so their policy
became as a matter of course the policy of the Institute. They
aspired to nothing less than the consolidation of all water colourists
worth taking into account at all into an united body, which should
do for this branch of practice what the Academy was doing for
oil painting. As a first step in this direction they secured a site
for a large gallery in which they proposed to hold exhibitions, like
those at Burlington House, open to all comers, and as a second step
they opened negotiations for an amalgamation with the " Old
Society," so as to ensure the co-operation of all the chief exponents
of the art. Had things gone exactly as they intended they would
certainly have brought about a remarkable combination abounding
with possibilities, and calculated to add some entirely new chapters
to the history of the school.

However, they failed to gain over the " Old Society " to their view,
though they made two attempts to induce that institution to consider the scheme favourably. The first proposition was embodied in
a letter sent by the President and Vice-President of the Institute at
the end of April, 1881, in which, after announcing that arrangements
had been practically completed " for securing galleries in which
exhibitions of water-colour art can be held on a large scale," they
proceeded to point out the advantages which were likely to accrue
from a junction of the two societies for the carrying out of the
project. To this letter an answer was returned about a week later
by the Secretary of the " Old Society," stating that a General
Meeting had been convened for the discussion of the matter ; and
after the lapse of a fortnight another communication was received

by the Institute, accompanied by a copy of the resolution passed at this meeting—"That the Society having considered a letter from the Institute of Painters in Water Colours proposing an amalgamation of the two Societies to take the projected new galleries to be erected by the 'Piccadilly Art Galleries Company, Limited,' the Council be directed to reply to the same respectfully declining such proposal."

The second proposition was made in March, 1882. During the interval a great deal of unofficial discussion had gone on, and representatives of both bodies—Sir J. D. Linton and Mr. J. Orrock for the Institute and Sir F. Powell and Mr. H. Wallis for the " Old Society "—had met to deliberate about the various questions which were likely to arise under the scheme of amalgamation and to examine together the plans of the new building. There had been, indeed, some misconceptions concerning the exact nature of the proposals of the Institute, but with fuller explanations the probability of a satisfactory settlement seemed to be increasing. Moreover, the younger association was prepared to make many concessions and to abandon certain of its own privileges to bring about the desired result, so that in renewing its overtures it was not merely trying to re-open a question which had been already settled.

In the 1882 letter a plain statement was provided of the points at issue between the two societies. It began by reference to the fact that there was in existence some misunderstanding as to the nature and scope of the proposal for amalgamation, and it suggested that to this misunderstanding was probably due the failure of the previous negotiation. On the ground that a serious endeavour was advisable " to discover whether the difficulties in the way of such a union are altogether insuperable " it proceeded next to deal with the most important obstacles — the name of the society, the question of accumulated property, and the disproportion between the numbers of the two societies. The first was to be settled by calling the united body the " Royal Society of Painters in Water Colours," the second by the provision of a guarantee fund by each society, and the third by the readiness of a large proportion of the Institute members to return to the rank of Associates if by so doing they could promote the desired combination. The letter concluded with a declaration that the scheme was inspired by " a sincere desire to advance the progress of water-colour art " and that the Institute, in the belief that the want of united action was a source of danger, was willing to make any reasonable concessions to put matters properly in order. This communication, like the first, was duly considered at a General

Assembly of the members of the " Old Society " held on April 25th, 1882, and on the same day the answer was returned, to the effect that—" The members of this Society, while recognising and acknowledging the friendly feeling shown in the proposal of the Institute, which they very sincerely reciprocate, regret that after mature consideration they have been led to the conclusion that the fusion or amalgamation of the two Societies presents difficulties of various kinds which they find to be insurmountable, and that consequently they are unable further to entertain the proposition which the Institute has done them the honour to make."

Apparently the idea which chiefly influenced the decision of the " Old Society " was that the financial responsibilities which would be brought upon the association by attempting such an ambitious undertaking would be unduly heavy, and that the results of the proposed exhibition would be insufficient to justify the inevitably large expenditure and increase of liabilities. The Members felt that they would be committing themselves to a course of action which would be a little too experimental, to a policy which would certainly be expensive and only possibly productive of an income which would cover the very serious outgoings. They refused not out of any ill-will for the Institute, not because they failed to sympathise with its desire to advance the interests of water-colour painting, but because they thought that these interests, and their own as well, would be best served by keeping things as they were. No doubt they realised that by refusing to participate they ran some risk of losing the leading position which they had held for so many years ; the success of the Institute scheme might quite possibly have destroyed a rival society which persisted in maintaining the tradition of close exhibitions. But they were willing to take this risk because it seemed less serious than the danger of being involved in financial responsibilities which would not be easy to control ; and on the whole their attitude has been justified by subsequent events.

For, though the Institute, reinforced by some thirty new Members, the men who had been active in the management of " The Dudley," proceeded with its scheme, and took possession of its new headquarters triumphantly, it was destined before long to experience a series of annoyances, which were due to strained relations with the Company that owned the building. At first, indeed, everything promised well. The galleries in Piccadilly were opened in April, 1883, with a brilliant ceremony, at which the King, then Prince of Wales, was present ; and in the inaugural exhibition, which consisted of eight hundred and ninety-nine drawings, sales to the

XX R 1

amount of some £14,000 were effected. Shortly after the opening of this Exhibition the association became, by command of Queen Victoria, the Royal Institute of Painters in Water Colours; and some two years later the President, J. D. Linton, who had been elected to this post in 1884, on the retirement of Louis Haghe after ten years' service, received the honour of knighthood. About the end of 1883 the Institute also made an attempt to establish free schools, more or less on the lines of those at the Royal Academy, for the teaching of water-colour painting; but these did not produce the results expected, and were eventually abandoned.

It was two or three years after the move from Pall Mall to Piccadilly that the dispute between the Institute and the Piccadilly Art Galleries Company became acute. The Company, the shares of which were held chiefly by members of the Institute, had erected the building at a cost of £60,000, upon a site a lease of which for a term of about eighty years had been obtained at a ground-rent of £2,000 a year. For the whole of this term the Institute was to be a tenant of the Company during certain months in each year, and was to be given a lease embodying these conditions; while the Company was to have possession of the galleries during the rest of the year, and to be at liberty to let them when they were not occupied by the Institute. When the delivery of this lease was demanded by the Institute, the Company refused to carry out the agreement, and proceedings to compel delivery were accordingly commenced in the Court of Chancery. The case was ultimately settled in Court, and a compromise was agreed to under which the Institute received a lease of the galleries for the period of the ground lease, and became responsible for the sub-letting to other tenants, and the company retained the remainder of the building. This compromise was negotiated by Sir J. D. Linton and Mr. Orrock, as the representatives of the artists who were members of the association; it defined the position of the Institute, but at the same time it imposed upon it a greater financial strain and increased the risks of its position. However, no better way out of the difficulty was to be found, and the settlement had at least the advantage of securing to the artists the full control of their exhibition rooms, and of preventing any danger of future disputes concerning their rights and privileges as a Society.

During the twenty years which have elapsed since this adjustment of the difficulties which threatened to greatly hamper the progress of the remodelled and reconstituted society, the Institute has carried on its work with a reasonable degree of success. That it has experienced its share of the vicissitudes which have in recent times affected the prosperity of all artistic associations can by no means be denied ; but it has maintained its authority, and has continued to serve the interests of the whole body of water-colour painters with dignity and discretion. Some changes have taken place in the constitution of the body, changes brought about by the death or secession of prominent members, and the Presidency has passed from Sir J. D. Linton (who resigned in 1898) to Mr. E. J. Gregory, whose name was first inscribed upon the roll of the Institute in 1871. But in all essentials the policy which was decided upon in the early eighties has remained unaltered, and any departure from it now seems unlikely. The lines upon which the Institute is conducted have been too definitely settled, and have been too well tested by prolonged experiment, to make probable a divergence from them in a new direction or a reversion to the traditions of a close society.

It is interesting to make some comparison between the character of the exhibitions for which the Institute has been responsible since its expansion and of those which have been arranged during the same period by the " Old Society." This comparison is legitimate, because these exhibitions represent points of view which are in some respects opposed. That both institutions are striving honestly for the maintenance of the art of water-colour painting in a condition of healthy activity, and for the encouragement of all workers in the medium who are sincere in their aims, is by no means to be disputed. But the " Old Society " adheres to the principle that the interests of the art are best served by shows made up entirely of the achievements of men of proved ability, who have as an essential preliminary to admission to its ranks demonstrated the justice of their claim to attention. It does not make experiments, and it does not open its galleries to immature or tentative effort. The result is that the collections it periodically brings together are a little formal, a little lacking in features that are novel or unexpected ; but, on the other hand, they are always distinguished and convincing. The people who go to see them can count with something like certainty upon finding an important gathering of accomplished and admirable work by artists with whose methods they are familiar, and upon being able to study the methods of some of the ablest living exponents of the technicalities of water-colour painting, and they can feel sure that the best traditions of the Society will be scrupulously respected.

The Institute, however strenuous its members may be in their

xxii R I

advocacy of the highest standard of water-colour practice, cannot ensure in its shows quite the same consistency of quality. It can, of course, always depend upon the contributions of a number of eminent artists to give to each exhibition a kind of nucleus, round which the works of less known men can be grouped ; but as its galleries are open to all water colourists of reasonable ability, anything approaching uniformity of merit is not to be expected. The more mature performances of the Members are juxtaposed with those of artists who are neither so sure of themselves nor so experienced in the management of the medium ; and, consequently, there is usually a much greater range of accomplishment in the periodical gatherings. That this range should be as wide as it can be made without unduly lowering the necessary standard of practice is an essential part of the policy of the Institute. No work of sufficiently good quality is likely to be refused, no matter how much it may depart from what the Members may privately consider to be the strict traditions of water-colour painting, because the mission of the gallery is not so much to uphold these traditions in their entirety as to provide a place in which water colourists with new ideas about the possibilities of their craft can put forward their appeal for public and professional attention. The visitor to the shows may be surprised at some of the work he finds in them—he may even be shocked if he is a rigid stickler for the more formal conventions— but he can go with the belief that he will almost always see something that will interest him legitimately and provide him with opportunities for instructive comparisons. He is practically sure to have some new sensations and to get some fresh impressions of the possibilities of the art which he desires to investigate.

If therefore the " Old Society " mainly presents what may be called the fullest development of water colour, and shows expressively the connection between present and past beliefs and methods, the Institute gives rather a suggestion of the manner in which present-day convictions will probably be modified in the future. In one sense the " Old Society " may be said to be always a little behind the times and its younger rival to be a little ahead of them ; yet both are essential for the proper building up of the history of an art that is particularly alive and eminently capable of being directed along new lines. The Institute is a sort of training ground, where fresh ideas and ambitions are tested and the value of conspicuous departures from precedent is appraised by men of experience. It has played, and is still playing, a part of much distinction in the evolution of our water-colour school, a part that imposes upon its members a large amount of responsibility and that calls for constant study of the changing conditions of the art world. In its desire to do its duty thoroughly, it has not hesitated to involve itself in serious liabilities and to assume obligations which impose a sufficiently severe tax upon its resources. But in this it shows its sincerity, and proves that it considers the realisation of its aims to be worth some sacrifices. If it had continued as a close society it would probably have enjoyed year by year a due measure of calm and uneventful success ; but it would have remained a kind of shadow of the " Old Society," and would have helped but little to encourage the progress of English water colour. Now, however, it is the recognised rallying place for all workers in the medium who are not already appropriated ; and in this capacity it is doing work that is as useful as it is honourable.

THE MEMBERS OF THE INSTITUTE

LTHOUGH it can scarcely be said that the Institute, when it was first brought into existence as the New Society of Painters in Water Colours, succeeded at once in obtaining the support of many of the men who are considered to-day to have a right to a place among the chiefs of our water-colour school, it is quite evident that the founders of the association were ambitious to rally round them a strong band of able artists. In the rather high-flown circular issued in 1831 to announce the inception of their undertaking, there is the fullest profession of various lofty aspirations which might fairly have been expected to claim the consideration of the best men in the profession. This circular declares that : " History affords ample testimony to show that the encouragement of the fine arts has been considered an object worthy the solicitude of the wise, the liberal, and the enlightened of every age and in all civilised nations. In those countries where they did not find a home all was gloom and tyranny and desolation ; in vain do we look for their bland and social influence under such ungenial systems : for it is only amongst a people whose institutions are founded in rational freedom, and who are sufficiently civilised to appreciate the value of mental cultivation, that the arts which adorn society have ever been cultivated with success ; and in return those arts educate the human intellect almost imperceptibly, improve the general taste, and make politeness of mind keep pace with refinement of manners.

" If, then, those distinctive marks of civilisation apply to the fine arts generally, it will be admitted that their application to painting in water-colours has a peculiar propriety. This truly British art is capable of being carried to a point much nearer perfection than it has yet attained ; but that great object can be effected only by a just and liberal course of proceeding—one under which its best interests would be promoted by affording to the unfriended talent of the country, equally with that of the established professor, a full and fair opportunity of publicly displaying itself without any restraint, except such as reason, good feeling, and impartial justice require. It is, therefore, solely upon the broad and simple principle of personal merit, that the New Society of Painters in Water Colours have made their appeal to the patrons and admirers of the arts ; and upon that basis are founded the laws and regulations for the government of the Society and the management of their Exhibitions."

This expression of the aims of the new society was signed by eight artists ; William Cowen, James Fuge, Thomas Maisey, Giles Firman Phillips, Joseph Powell, George Sidney Shepherd, William B. Sarsfield Taylor, and Thomas Wageman, who as Foundation Members organised and arranged the first exhibition held in the spring of 1832. They received a very full measure of support for, as has been already recorded, the show included over three hundred works contributed by some hundred and twenty artists, and was so far successful financially that there remained, after the expenses had been defrayed, a small balance in the hands of the treasurer.

In the preface to the catalogue of this exhibition a further declaration of policy was made, which may be quoted because it shows the grounds on which were based the expectations of the men who were actively promoting the scheme of the society. "The art of painting in water-colours," it runs, "as it is now practised, may justly be said to be the creation of British genius. In no other part of the world has this branch of the fine arts approached the excellence which it has reached in this country. To this fact is attributable the deserved success and popularity of the Society of Painters in Water Colours. The number of the members of that Society is, however, limited ; and although, at the period of its establishment, that number probably comprehended a majority of the ablest water-colour painters in the kingdom, such is far from being the case at present ; as a proof of which there are every year numerous applications for admission into the Society of Painters in Water Colours which are rejected, simply because there are not any vacancies and not on the ground of any want of qualification in the applicants. It is nevertheless well known that at present there is no place in the metropolis in which paintings in water colours are exhibited to advantage but in the gallery of that Society.

"Under these circumstances, many professors of water-colour painting in its various departments are impressed with the conviction that no mode remains to them of bringing their works fairly before the public but by the formation of a New Society. They are persuaded that there is ample room for two Societies ; and that there is abundant talent in the country to furnish an additional annual exhibition, the merit of which will entitle it to the encouragement of the public. To form this institution on a liberal and extended plan—to diffuse its advantages as widely as possible, and to produce a greater variety of talent, it is proposed to extend the number of exhibitors and merely to limit the number of works sent in by each painter."

The essential point of difference between the New Society and the older institution with which it proposed to enter into competition is plainly asserted in this last sentence. The actual members were not to be, as they were, and still are, in the " Old Society," the sole contributors to the exhibitions, but were to act as a kind of managing committee and be responsible for maintaining a proper standard of quality in the shows to be brought together. This probably accounts for the comparatively small membership of the New Society during the first three or four years of its career. It began, as has been already mentioned, with only eight Members, it had nineteen in 1833, twenty-one in 1834, and twenty-eight in 1835, the year in which it decided to change its constitution and become a close society. After that the increase was more marked ; and in 1842, ten years after the opening of the first exhibition, the total amounted to forty-eight.

How anxious the Society was to gather round it as many outside supporters as possible can be inferred from the tone of the preface— or " Address," as it is called—to the 1833 catalogue, when it had changed its name to " The Associated Painters in Water Colours." This change, for some occult reason, was assumed to be likely to advance the interests of the association—" In submitting to the Patrons and Professors of Art this Second Annual Exhibition of Paintings in Water Colours, the committee feel it necessary to state that for the extension of its advantages, in a professional point of view, and to render its character less limited and more national, the designation of the exhibition will, in future, be that of " The Associated Painters in Water Colours," under which designation the privileges possessed by donors, or subscribers, will be preserved as originally established.

" The formation of the Association having arisen out of the great necessity that was found to exist for extending the means by which men of talent may have a fair opportunity of bringing their works advantageously before the public, and thus be enabled to share in that patronage so liberally bestowed on this branch of the fine arts— the regulations, as to professors, will continue to be such as to offer every facility for the exhibition of their works. It is only upon the broad and simple principle of personal merit that this Institution has been founded, and its regulations formed ; and it being, therefore, solely by the talent displayed in his works that the artist can claim any preference—men of real merit, hitherto kept in comparative obscurity, and unknown to the public, will thus receive equal attention, and will have an opportunity of displaying their drawings without any restraint, except such as reason, good feeling, and impartial justice require.

" The degree of interest that is felt in the most exalted and influential portion of society for the successful cultivation and improvement of an art universally acknowledged to owe its present perfection to British genius is sufficiently evidenced by the Royal and noble patronage with which this Association has been honoured, and it is under these highly favourable auspices that the promoters of the exhibition presume respectfully to solicit the encouragement of those who may feel anxious for the prosperity of an Institution founded, as this avowedly is, on truly liberal principles."

Some hint, however, that things were not going quite smoothly with the Society is given in the circular issued on February 28th, 1834, to announce the completion of the arrangements for that year's exhibition :—" The Committee beg leave most respectfully to call the attention of the nobility and gentry to the Third Annual Exhibition of the New Society of Painters in Water Colours ; and in returning their sincere thanks for the flattering support that has been already afforded them, they most earnestly solicit the continuance and extension of the same generous patronage to the ensuing exhibition, which will be opened to the public on Monday, the 7th of April next. In conducting the affairs of the above Society many difficulties have arisen which have happily been surmounted ; and the Committee feel great pride in directing public attention to the only institution which affords an ample opportunity for the rising talent of the day to develop itself in this truly English department of the arts. That such a Society had long been a desideratum must be obvious to all from the well known exclusion, from the original one, of all works (however talented) not executed by its own members, it being a distinguishing feature in the Regulations of the New Society — that every artist in the United Kingdom is eligible to become a member or exhibitor."

These admitted " difficulties " refer presumably to the internal dissensions mentioned in the previous chapter. They seem to have caused an astonishing number of changes in the constitution of the body of men who were responsible members of the Society and directed its affairs. For example, of the eight artists who signed the 1831 circular and managed the first exhibition in 1832, four disappeared in 1833—Cowen, Fuge, Sarsfield Taylor and Wageman. For the 1833 exhibition fifteen new members joined the four who remained : A. Clint, J. M. Burbank, T. Wood, M. Macpherson, R. W. Buss, E. J. Pasquier, T. Lindsay, A. Martin, E. Duncan, T. S. Cooper, J. Noblett, G. Chambers, W. H. Kearney, W. H. Bach, and G. Scharf ; and of these, Clint, Wood, Buss, Martin, Duncan, Cooper, and Chambers had gone before the opening of the 1834 show. The newcomers in that year were W. N. Hardwick, V. Bartholomew, H. P. Rivière, H. E. Downing, J. A. Cahusac, W. Hudson, J. Burgess, James Fahey, B. R. Green, John Chase, and Thomas Dunage, and three of these, Bartholomew, Burgess and Dunage, with Pasquier, Bach, Macpherson, Powell, and Burbank, do not figure in the list for 1835. Chambers and Bartholomew were elected Associates of the "Old Society" in 1834 and 1835 respectively.

Immediately after the closing of the 1834 exhibition, the radical change in the policy of the Society seems to have been decided upon. The nature of this change is set forth in a manuscript in the possession of the Institute :—"The undersigned gentlemen do hereby agree to unite together for the purpose of remodelling the New Society of Painters in Water Colours upon the understanding that none but responsible members shall be exhibitors, and that they agree to share equally the expenses and labours necessary for the same." To this document are appended the names of B. R. Green, G. S. Shepherd, W. N. Hardwick, W. H. Kearney, H. E. Downing, J. M. Burbank, G. Scharf, J. A. Cahusac, J. Burgess, Thomas Lindsay, James Fahey, Thomas Maisey, and John Chase, already Members of the Society, and those of three new men, G. B. Campion, G. H. Laporte, and Gordon Bradley, who now appear for the first time. In the interval between the preparation of this agreement—which is dated July 29th, 1834—and the opening of the 1835 exhibition, several additions were made to the list. Duncan came in again, and with him Hudson, Noblett, and Rivière, who were members under the old condition of affairs ; and a number of new people were elected—T. A. Firminger, Louis Haghe, G. Howse, W. Oliver, F. Rochard, G. Sims, C. H. Weigall, Miss Laporte, Mrs. Harrison, and Miss M. A. Rix. Burbank and Burgess, though they signed the agreement, did not continue to belong to the Society.

Such a complete change in the scheme of "an institution founded, as this avowedly is, on truly liberal principles," called for some

R I xxix

explanation. So in September, 1834, was issued a kind of manifesto, giving the reasons for the departure :—

" Several important alterations having taken place in the laws of this Society, the committee beg to lay before the members of the profession a statement of the circumstances which have called for a remodelling of its constitution.

" The object of the Association was, it will be remembered, to provide a gallery for works in this department of art, where they might be brought before the public eye without the injury to their effect experienced in other exhibitions, by an injudicious collision with paintings in oil.

" The gradual improvement in the exhibitions of this Institution during three seasons, notwithstanding many serious difficulties experienced by its first supporters, warrants its members confidently to hope it may ultimately acquire a character as high, and stand upon a basis as firm, as that which has so long enjoyed the public favour.

" Hitherto, however, not only the management, but the entire responsibility has rested with a few individuals, and through their means facilities have been given for a public inspection of works of talent, by which many artists have risen to an eminent rank in their profession, who were before comparatively unknown to the public. This having been effected, it was reasonably hoped that gentlemen who had derived benefits from the Association would have readily come forward to contribute their aid towards its support—even if actuated by no other motive than individual interest ; but these expectations have not been realised.

" Another evil, which, if not provided against, must prove fatal to the Society, is the fact that so long as artists, whose views are directed towards the senior Society, and who from year to year offer themselves as candidates for election there, can elsewhere find a place in which to exhibit their works without even contributing to the funds necessary for its continuance—it is to be lamented, but cannot be denied, that persons will be found who are no further interested in the prosperity of the Association than as affording them a means of present advantage.

" Thus, whilst the energies of a few are constantly directed to the firm establishment of a society for the furtherance of art and benefit of its professors, they are continually liable to be deprived of such artists at the very time when they had become really valuable contributors to the annual exhibitions, a deprivation effected designedly for the purpose of crushing that honourable spirit of emulation which should characterise all liberal institutions.

XXX R I

" It was, in consequence, resolved at a meeting held in July last, as the only course to be pursued, that artists interested in the welfare and future stability of this Institution should incorporate themselves into a society, the members of which should share equally in the management and pecuniary responsibility.

" The committee beg to state that it is far from the intention of the Society to depart from those principles of liberality which prompted them to open their doors to the admission of talent; on the contrary—though they feel an urgent necessity for such a reformation of their laws as shall place the Society upon a permanent foundation—they invite all artists of talent desirous of exhibiting their productions, to become members, and thereby share equally in the advantages accruing from it."

To this rather long-winded circular, with its sufficiently definite exposition of the reasons which induced the New Society to turn its back upon its earlier principles, are appended certain extracts from the laws, "subjoined for the information of gentlemen desirous of becoming members." The chief of these extracts are:—" That the Society shall consist of an unlimited number of members"; "That all artists of talent are eligible to become members"; "That the expenses of the Society shall be borne equally by every member"; and "That each member shall become bound to the President to forfeit the sum of twenty guineas on leaving the Society without the consent of its members." This last regulation was clearly intended to check the tendency, "to be lamented" but recognized as inevitable, on the part of exhibitors with the younger association to use the publicity they gained there as a help to admission into the "Old Society." It was no doubt inspired by the defection of Chambers and Bartholomew, and by the fact that other men like J. Nash, C. Bentley, and James Holland, who had been extensive contributors to the first few exhibitions of the New Society, had been almost immediately gathered in by its rival.

The effect of this change of constitution was to increase at once the stability of the institution and to diminish the withdrawals of Members to an appreciable extent. But, despite the twenty-guinea fine, the periodical secessions were still inconveniently numerous— for instance Noblett and Hudson resigned in 1835, Scharf in 1836, and Bradley, Morison, Cahusac, and J. Martin in 1838—and a good many new men had to be elected to keep the concern in proper working order. In 1836 there came in John Martin, Douglas Morison, J. Newton, R. Kyrke Penson, and W. Robertson; and of these Morison only exhibited twice—in the exhibitions for 1836 and

1837—and Martin once, in 1837, as a member, and once, in 1838, as an invited contributor. According to the roll of the Institute, J. M. Tayler was also elected in 1836, but, if so, he must have withdrawn immediately, for his name does not appear in the catalogues, and he did not contribute to the exhibitions. The same can be said of John Gilbert, who is included with Lilburne Hicks, Thomas Kearnan, Edward Henry Wehnert, and Miss Louisa Corbaux in the list of members added in 1837; he certainly took no part in the affairs of the society.

Some evidence of the steady progress in the prestige of the New Society, and of the increasing readiness to join it on the part of artists of notable ability, was afforded by the 1838 elections. The successful candidates were Aaron Penley, " Painter in Water Colours to Her Majesty the Queen Dowager," John Skinner Prout, the nephew of the more famous Samuel Prout and the friend of William Muller, John Absolon, Henry Johnston, and Edward H. Corbould, an able painter of historical subjects who was destined to remain a Member of the Society for nearly seventy years. Prout exhibited drawings in 1839 and 1840, and then went to live in Australia; so his name was removed from the list on account of his inability to contribute to the exhibitions. He was, however, re-elected on his return to England in 1849, and he retained his membership until his death in 1876. Johnston left the Society in 1842.

Five new Members were elected in 1839; Henry Bright, Thomas S. Robins, Alfred H. Taylor, William Telbin, and Miss Fanny Corbaux, who had shown drawings in the two previous years as an invited exhibitor. In this year a change was made in the Presidency of the New Society. Its first President had been Joseph Powell, who died in 1834. He had been succeeded by Thomas Maisey—" the man named, Maisey, who," according to Sarsfield Taylor, " had usurped the office of President "—and in 1839 Henry Warren was chosen to fill the post. The change may have been due to Maisey's failing health, for he died in the following year, but the passage quoted in the previous chapter from Sarsfield Taylor's book certainly implies that the appointment of Warren was a consequence of some sort of revolt on the part of the newcomers in the Society against the authority of a President with whose methods they were not in agreement. At all events Maisey's deposition did not cause him to resign his membership; his name appears in the Members' list in both the 1839 and 1840 exhibitions. Warren held office for thirty years, and resigned in

1873 on the ground of increasing age and infirmity; but he remained Honorary President of the Institute till his death in 1879. The change made in the rules of the Society in 1840 has been previously mentioned; hitherto the candidates for admission had become full Members immediately on election, and had at once assumed their share of responsibility in the management of the affairs of the association. But in 1840 an Associate class was created, and thenceforward for nearly thirty years all new-comers had to be received into this preliminary class before they could be advanced to actual membership. The responsible Members in this year numbered thirty-four—John Absolon, H. Bright, G. B. Campion, Vice-President, J. Chase, E. H. Corbould, E. Duncan, T. A. Firminger, B. R. Green, L. Haghe, W. N. Hardwick, L. Hicks, G. Howse, Henry Johnston, T. Kearnan, W. H. Kearney, G. H. Laporte, T. Lindsay, T. Maisey, W. Oliver, A. Penley, R. K. Penson, J. S. Prout, H. P. Rivière, W. Robertson, T. S. Robins, F. Rochard, G. S. Shepherd, G. Sims, A. H. Taylor, W. Telbin, Henry Warren, the president, E. H. Wehnert, C. H. Weigall, treasurer, and James Fahey, secretary; and there were besides four lady Members—Miss F. Corbaux, Miss L. Corbaux, Miss Laporte, and Mrs. Harrison, who did not participate in the working of the Society, and did not incur any financial obligations.

To this list were added in 1840 five Associates—Thomas Shotter Boys and W. Knight Keeling, who were both promoted to membership in the following year; O. W. Brierley and Thomas Miles Richardson, who retired together in 1843; and F. J. D'Egville. Richardson became immediately an Associate of the "Old Society," into which Brierley was also received nearly thirty years later. The elections in 1841 were David Cox, Jun., Henry Maplestone, J. M. Youngman, and Miss Sarah Setchel; and in 1842 John Wykeham Archer, George Haydock Dodgson, J. J. Jenkins, Francis William Topham, and Mrs. Margetts. It may be noted that though all these—the lady Members excepted—were elected as Associates, no distinction is made between the two classes of contributors in the catalogues of the exhibitions at this period. All the names are included in one list of "Members."

It would seem that the "New Society" had attained a position of reasonable authority, and had no need to seek for any large number of new contributors to strengthen its hold upon the public; for there comes now a short period during which few elections were made; there was one, of Henry Jutsum, in 1843, none in 1844, and three, John Callow, William Lee, and Miss Jane Sophia

Egerton, in 1845. A marked and gratifying improvement in its popularity is implied also by the record of the sales in the exhibitions held during the years which followed closely on the change in the constitution of the Society. In 1838 the total amount realised was only £385 7s. 0d., in 1839 it rose to £739 1s. 6d., in 1840 to £762 12s. 6d., in 1841 to £1,277 12s. 0d., and in 1842 it reached the respectable sum of £1,990 16s. 0d. This progressive increase may be taken as proof that in the ten years that had elapsed since the first exhibition was held the development of the institution had been sufficiently continuous, and that the popular appreciation of its efforts had steadily grown wider and more efficient.

But this happy condition of affairs did not last long. In 1845 began the series of resignations which deprived the Society of some of its best supporters. Bright went in that year, Miss Laporte, and David Cox, Junr., in 1846, Duncan, Jenkins, Dodgson, and Topham, in 1847, and Jutsum and Callow in 1848 ; a group of able artists whose importance was proved by the readiness of the " Old Society " to absorb nearly all of them without loss of time. Cox, Duncan, Dodgson, and Topham, were elected Associates of the rival institution in 1848, Callow and Jenkins in 1849. Things were not going well with the younger society at that moment ; there were clearly matters on which the members could not agree, and the minority preferred resignation to compromise.

However, there does not seem to have been any difficulty great enough to deter other artists from joining the New Society. The vacant places were filled by the election of William Collingwood, H. C. Pidgeon, Charles Vacher, Miss Fanny Rosenberg, and Miss Fanny Steers, in 1846 ; Charles Davidson, John Henry Mole, and Henry Theobald, in 1847 ; William Bennett, Robert Carrick, Michael Angelo Hayes, D. H. McKewan, and T. L. Rowbotham, in 1848 ; and Samuel Cook, Harrison Weir, W. Wyld, and Mrs. William Oliver, in 1849. Davidson and Collingwood resigned in 1853 and 1854 respectively, and joined the " Old Society " in 1855.

During the next sixteen years—from the end of 1849 to 1866—only twenty-eight additions were made to the list. In 1850 came the election of Thomas H. Cromek, in 1852 those of A. J. Bouvier and E. G. Warren, in 1854 those of Charles Brocky, Philip Mitchell, J. W. Whymper, and Miss Emily Farmer ; but there were none in 1851, 1853, or 1855. Only one candidate, James G. Philp, was successful in 1856, and one other, Thomas Sutcliffe, in 1857.

Then the number of elections began to increase again ; Edward Morin, G. A. Simonoau, and Henry F. Tidey came in 1855 ; Joseph M. Jopling and Edward Richardson, in 1859 ; Edwin Hayes, the sea-painter whose death is a matter of quite recent memory, and Carl Werner, in 1860 ; Joseph Charles Reed, Mrs. William Duffield, and Mrs. Henry Murray, in 1861 ; William Wood Deane, who went over to the " Old Society " in 1870, and W. Leighton Leitch, in 1862 ; Charles Cattermole, Henry G. Hine, and George Shalders, in 1863 ; and in 1864 Charles Green, William Lucas, and William Luson Thomas, who afterwards as organiser and editor of *The Graphic* rendered services of the utmost value to illustrated journalism, and gave to a host of able black-and-white draughtsmen opportunities of inestimable importance. In 1865 a single election took place, that of Guido R. Bach, a very able painter of historical and romantic subjects.

The list of names for 1866 is swelled by the addition of three Honorary Members, Rosa Bonheur, Louis Gallait, and J. B. Madou, the President of the Royal Belgian Society of Painters in Water-Colours ; the Associates elected in the ordinary manner were G. G. Kilburne, John Mogford, John Sherrin, and L. J. Wood. In the following year more Honorary Members were chosen—Madame Henriette Browne, F. Goodall, R.A., J. R. Herbert, R.A., Daniel Maclise, R.A., Sir John Millais, R.A., and J. L. E. Meissonier—and six Associates, R. Beavis, Edward Hargitt, J. T. Hixon, James Mahony, Henry B. Roberts, and James Drumgole Linton, the future President of the society. This rapid rate of increase in the number of admissions was not, however, maintained, there were only three elections, of Valentine Walter Bromley, H. J. Johnson, and Andrew C. Gow—now a Member of the Royal Academy—in 1868 ; and none in 1869.

Three artists of unquestionable distinction—Thomas Collier, one of our greatest masters of water-colour painting, Edward H. Fahey, a sincere and accomplished student of nature, and William Small, a famous illustrator—joined the Institute in 1870 ; and six others in 1871, Hugh Carter, W. W. May, James Orrock, F. J. Skill, Hubert Herkomer, and E. J. Gregory, the last two of whom are now Royal Academicians. Professor von Herkomer, as he must be called to-day, left the Institute in 1890, and is a Member of the " Old Society," but Mr. Gregory has remained and fills the office of President, to which he succeeded on the resignation of Sir J. D. Linton in 1898. One election took place in 1872, of Josef

Israels as an Honorary Member, and one in 1873, of E. M. Wimperis as an Associate.

This momentary pause in the elections was amply made up for in the following year when eight Associates were admitted. They were James Hardy, John A. Houston, a member of the Royal Scottish Academy, William Simpson, John Syer, Joseph Wolf, the animal painter, Sir John Tenniel, the famous *Punch* cartoonist, Miss Elizabeth Thompson, better known as Lady Butler, and J. W. Oakes, who resigned in 1875, and was immediately after elected an Associate of the Royal Academy. Lady Butler left the Institute in 1878. Three more lady Members were added in 1875, Mrs. H. Coleman Angell, Miss Marian Chase, and Miss Mary Gow ; and three Associates, Towneley Green, C. E. Holloway, and C. J. Staniland. Four distinguished artists were elected in 1876, James Aumonier, Edwin Bale, George Clausen, and J. Seymour Lucas, all of whom are counted among the most popular and accomplished of living workers. The first two have remained Members of the Institute, but Mr. Seymour Lucas and Mr. Clausen retired respectively in 1888 and 1886, and are now Members of the Royal Academy. Mr. Seymour Lucas did not leave the Institute on his election as an Associate of the Academy : he deferred his resignation for two years after his entry into Burlington House. There was also one Honorary Member appointed in 1876, E. M. Ward, R.A., the popular painter of historical pictures. As the abolition of the Associates was decided upon in 1879, only four other candidates were required to pass into the Institute through the junior grade, T. Walter Wilson in 1877, and John Fulleylove, Harry Hine, and Paul Falconer Poole, R.A., in 1878. The first three of these, of course, became full Members in 1879, but Poole, presumably as a consequence of his eminence among the artists of his time, was made a Member in the same year that he received the Associateship.

Comparatively few additions were made to the list of Members during the three years in which the Institute was busy with its scheme for building its new galleries in Piccadilly and with its preparation for the great extension of its responsibilities which was to be undertaken as soon as these galleries were completed. There were five elections in 1879, of Henry J. Stock, F. W. W. Topham, Sir Coutts Lindsay, Lady Lindsay of Balcarres, and G. H. Boughton, who, in the same year, was chosen an Associate of the Royal Academy ; one, in 1880, of Lionel P. Smythe ; and one, of Mark Fisher, in 1881. The Empress Frederick of Germany consented to become an Honorary Member in 1880. As so large an increase in the membership was immediately impending, this temporary falling off in the number of accepted candidates cannot be considered surprising ; it was nothing more than a momentary pause before a very vigorous move forward.

By this move—the election of practically all the men who had been associated with " The Dudley " and had managed the successful exhibitions in that gallery—the roll of male Members was raised from sixty-four, the total in 1881, to eighty-nine in 1882. Twenty-seven artists, all men of repute and distinguished capacity, came into the Society together, and with them three Honorary Members, Princess Henry of Battenberg, Dr. Edward Hamilton, and Spencer Vincent. There were, however, two resignations in 1882, of W. Lucas and R. Beavis, who had belonged to the Institute since 1864 and 1867 respectively. The twenty-seven new names make a quite imposing list ; Charles R. Aston, Randolph Caldecott, F. G. Cotman, Walter Crane, Frank Dillon, Charles Earle, George S. Elgood, Keeley Halswelle, Colin Hunter, C. E. Johnson, Joseph Knight, Charles J. Lewis, R. W. Macbeth, Thomas R. Macquoid, Percy Macquoid, J. T. Hamilton Macallum, J. MacWhirter, Alfred Parsons, Henry Pilleau, J. I. Richardson, Arthur Severn, Arthur Stocks, Frank Walton, J. W. Waterhouse, John White, R. Caton Woodville, and W. L. Wyllie. Among these was a former Associate of the " Old Society," Mr. Macbeth : he resigned his membership of the Institute in 1891, and was re-admitted into the " Old Society " in 1895.

As the limit of Members—which had under the new scheme been fixed at a hundred—was not reached even after this comprehensive election, there were added in 1883 Edwin A. Abbey, Thomas Huson, Walter Langley, Ludwig Passini, R. Spencer Stanhope, and George F. Wetherbee ; in 1884, Frank Dadd, C. Napier Hemy, and H. R. Steer, with Count Gleichen as an Honorary Member ; and in 1885, Hector Caffieri, Thomas Pyne, John Scott, W. H. Weatherhead, and another Honorary Member, Edward Combes, C.M.G. About the same rate of increase was maintained to the end of the eighties ; there were J. C. Dollman, Claude Hayes, Joseph Nash, and Madame Teresa Hegg de Landerset, with two Honorary Members, Prince Louis of Battenberg and Count Seckendorff, in 1886 ; Alfred East, Cyrus Johnson, Yeend King, John O'Connor, A. W. Weedon, Miss Jane M. Dealy, and Miss Annie M. Youngman in 1887 ; T. Austen Brown, Bernard Evans, William Hatherell, Jules Lessore, W. Barnes Wollen, Miss Alice

M. Hobson, Miss Alice Squire, and one Honorary Member, Sir James C. Harris, K.C.V.O., in 1888 ; and in 1889 Joshua Anderson Hague, Carlton A. Smith, Miss Kate Mary Whitley, and Miss Kate Greenaway.

But during this period there was a fairly considerable number of resignations. Lady Butler and Mrs. Coleman Angell had gone in 1878, and, as has been already mentioned, R. Beavis and W. Lucas in 1882. C. Werner went in 1883 ; H. B. Roberts and J. M. Youngman, both Members of many years' standing, went in 1884 ; G. H. Boughton in 1885 ; W. Small, Mark Fisher, Walter Crane, with George Clausen, in 1886 ; L. J. Wood, J. MacWhirter, C. Napier Hemy, and J. Seymour Lucas in 1888 ; A. C. Gow, Colin Hunter, and J. W. Waterhouse in 1889 ; and in 1890 the Institute lost Professor von Herkomer and Lionel Smythe. Several of these seceders joined the " Old Society "—Mrs. Angell in 1879, Beavis in 1882, Walter Crane in 1888, Clausen in 1889, Napier Hemy in 1890, Lionel Smythe in 1892, and Professor von Herkomer in 1893. To complete this list it may be mentioned here that the same transference has since been made by E. A. Abbey, who left the Institute in 1893, and went into the " Old Society " in 1895, and by Alfred Parsons, who left in 1898 and was received into the other association in 1899.

After 1889 there was for a while a diminution in the admissions of new Members, probably because by then the limit of numbers had been so nearly reached that there was no need of any special effort to keep the Institute at something like its full strength. No election took place in 1890 ; there were four, of Edgar Bundy, Robert Fowler, William Rainey, and Max Ludby, in 1891 ; four, of Charles M. Grierson, St. George Hare, George Sheridan Knowles, and R. B. Nisbet, in 1892 ; three, of J. Lucien Davis, Henry M. Rheam, and J. Leslie Thomson, and of Alfred Gilbert, R.A., as an Honorary Member, in 1893 ; one, of Madame Henriette Ronner, in 1894 ; and none in 1895, in which year there was, however, added one Honorary Member, B. J. Ottewell.

Then followed three unusually busy years, during which not less than thirty artists of unquestionable capacity and of very varied conviction were chosen. Six of them, Gordon F. Browne, Arthur A. Burrington, Edward Davies, Albert Kinsley, J. Bernard Partridge, Miss Gertrude Demain Hammond, and one Honorary Member, Professor Hans von Bartels, were elected in 1896 ; fourteen, W. D. Almond, W. W. Collins, F. W. Davis, David G. Green, John P. Gulich, Dudley Hardy, Phil May, Mortimer

xxxviii R I

Menpes, A. D. Peppercorn, John R. Reid, F. Stuart Richardson, Charles P. Sainton, J. H. Swanwick, and Hugh Thomson, in 1897 ; and nine, J. Shaw Crompton, G. S. Ferrier, J. Finnemore, W. Lee Hankey, J. S. Hill, R. G. Meyerheim, John Pedder, Henry Ryland, and J. Byam Shaw, in 1898. The same rate was not maintained in 1899, for in that year only two candidates were successful—Edward C. Clifford and Alexander MacBride. The large number of elections during the latter half of the nineties was probably due to the fact that a great many gaps were made at or about this time in the ranks of the Institute by deaths, as well as by the resignations already recorded. Thomas Collier and Keeley Halswelle died in 1891 ; Jules Lessore and C. J. Lewis in 1892 ; Charles Earle in 1893 ; Miss Setchel in 1894 ; H. G. Hine and Edward Hargitt in 1895 ; W. W. May, P. Mitchell, Hamilton Macallum, and J. Sherrin in 1896 ; C. E. Holloway in 1897 ; Charles Green and J. P. Gulich in 1898 ; and Towneley Green, William Simpson, and Joseph Wolf in 1899. Really very little more was done than was necessary to keep the Institute at something approaching its full strength.

Since 1899 the introduction of new Members has continued regularly, but the number in any one year has been never more than five. There were four in 1900, Charles E. Dixon, Henry W. L. Hurst—better known as Hal Hurst—Claude A. Shepperson, and A. Winter-Shaw ; five in 1901, Thomas Arthur Browne, who is generally described as Tom Browne, George C. Haité, John Hassall, Cecil J. Hobson, and Horatio Walker ; none in 1902 ; four in 1903, James Clark, Graham Petrie, Frank Reynolds, and J. Sanderson Wells ; one only, Terrick Williams, in 1904 ; and two, Christopher Clark and Alfred J. Munnings, in 1905. During this period again the elections have only just balanced the losses sustained by deaths and resignations. The deaths have been Charles Cattermole, E. M. Wimperis, and W. L. Thomas, in 1900 ; Madame Henriette Browne and Miss Kate Greenaway, in 1901 ; J. W. Whymper in 1902 ; Ludwig Passini and Phil May in 1903 ; Edwin Hayes in 1904, and E. H. Corbould in 1905 ; and the resignations have been T. Austen Brown and Hugh Carter in 1899, C. R. Aston and J. C. Dollman in 1901, and A. D. Peppercorn, W. H. Weatherhead, and Miss Gow in 1903. For the sake of completeness, it may be mentioned that before 1899 the Institute had lost by resignation two other distinguished Members, Mr. Wyllie in 1894, and Mr. East in 1898.

A comparison of the Members list in 1883, when the Institute had absorbed "The Dudley" and had established itself in its new quarters in Piccadilly, with that of 1905, is not without interest, for it shows that a quite considerable proportion of the men who did so much to put the reconstructed society on a sound footing are still active in its affairs. These survivors of the eighty-seven Members who had been gathered together in 1883 are E. J. Gregory, the President, J. Aumonier, John Fulleylove, H. J. Stock, Edwin Bale, F. G. Cotman, Frank Dillon, George S. Elgood, E. H. Fahey, Harry Hine, C. E. Johnson, G. G. Kilburne, Joseph Knight, Sir Coutts Lindsay, Sir J. D. Linton, Percy Macquoid, Thomas R. Macquoid, James Orrock, John I. Richardson, C. J. Staniland, F. W. W. Topham, Frank Walton, Edmund G. Warren, John White, and Sir John Tenniel, who became an Honorary Member at the end of 1904. Of the lady Members three only remained in 1905, Mrs. W. Duffield, Miss Emily Farmer, and Lady Lindsay, and one of these, Miss Farmer, has since died ; and of the Honorary Members there are two left, Princess Henry of Battenberg and Josef Israels. For further comparison it may be noted that in 1883 there were eighty-seven acting Members, twelve lady Members, and ten Honorary Members ; the numbers in 1905 were ninety-five, eleven, and eight respectively.

It can certainly be claimed for the Institute that during its career of more than seventy years it has at one time or another been able to count among its members a great many of the most accomplished painters of the British school. In a large number of instances it was the first of our art institutions to recognise the abilities of men who were making their way towards the front rank, and it did much to help these men onwards in their struggle for popular approval by publicly endorsing their appeal for attention from the public. Even in the fact that many of its supporters were periodically taken away by the "Old Society" and the Royal Academy—though no doubt the experience was annoying and to some extent disheartening—can be found a kind of practical admission that the Institute was encouraging the right type of art worker. If it had not chosen wisely the artists whom it was prepared to include in its own body of members, it would not have been used so persistently as a half-way house to other societies which had the advantage in seniority and in the prestige that comes from prolonged maintenance of a particular set of traditions. Moreover, the readiness of these other societies to draw away men from its ranks, or to gather in seceders who had left for reasons of their own, is plain proof that the Institute was in the habit of selecting a majority, at least, of the artists who were worthy of consideration. It did not leave unattached sufficient of them to satisfy the demands of the competing institutions, and if it had been able to retain all the men it appropriated it would quite conceivably have perceptibly reduced the authority of its rivals by cutting off to a great extent their supply of suitable recruits.

From the list of over three hundred men and women whose names have been inscribed upon its roll since the New Society made its first appearance in 1832—a list, by the way, which exceeds by nearly a hundred that of the "Old Society," despite its additional twenty-seven years of life—it would be possible to make a selection imposing both in the number and the importance of the individuals recorded. It would include—without drawing upon the Honorary Members—such notable artists among the earlier members of our water-colour school as Edward Duncan, George Chambers, Aaron Penley, J. S. Prout, T. M. Richardson, G. H. Dodgson, F. W. Topham, William Bennett, T. L. Rowbotham, D. H. McKewan, A. J. Bouvier, J. W. Whymper, John Callow, Charles Davidson, and Harrison Weir ; and among the more recent masters of the medium who are no longer living, men of acknowledged eminence like Edwin Hayes, H. G. Hine, Charles Green, Guido Bach, Thomas Collier, E. M. Wimperis, J. W. Oakes, Joseph Wolf, C. E. Holloway, G. H. Boughton, Randolph Caldecott, Hamilton Macallum, and John P. Gulich, besides Mrs. Coleman Angell and Miss Kate Greenaway. In the array of living Members can be counted many of the painters whom to-day we reckon as leaders in their profession. There are, for instance, Mr. Gregory and Sir J. D. Linton, veritable masters of delicate and highly finished water-colour ; Mr. A. W. Weedon, Mr. Aumonier, Mr. Leslie Thomson, Mr. F. G. Cotman, Mr. Frank Walton, Mr. Claude Hayes, Mr. Yeend King, Mr. G. C. Haité, Mr. R. B. Nisbet, Mr. Fulleylove, Mr. G. S. Elgood, Mr. Bernard Evans, Mr. Macbride, and Mr. J. S. Hill, all landscape painters of exceptional capacity ; and draughtsmen of the figure like Mr. Edgar Bundy, Mr. Robert Fowler, Mr. St. George Hare, Mr. Dudley Hardy, Mr. Wetherbee, Mr. Lee Hankey, Mr. Tom Browne, Mr. James Clark, Mr. John Hassall, and Mr. Byam Shaw, whose position in our art world is wholly beyond question—and all of these are actual contributors to the exhibitions of the Institute.

But besides the artists who are Members to-day there would have to be added to the record which proves how the Institute has carried on its work the names of many other living artists, past Members who have gone elsewhere—Mr. E. A. Abbey, Mr. Parsons, Mr. J. W. Waterhouse, Mr. A. C. Gow, Professor von Herkomer, Mr. Clausen, Mr. Seymour Lucas, Mr. Lionel Smythe, Mr. Wyllie, Mr. Walter Crane, Mr. Napier Hemy, Mr. East, Mr. MacWhirter, and Mr. Macbeth, who may not unfairly be said to have been helped by the Society to take the places in the world to which they were entitled by their merits. When in years to come the art history of our time is written by chroniclers who will judge recorded events with the impartiality born of remoteness from the strivings of the period with which they are dealing, it will certainly be counted to the credit of the Institute that it should have been so ready to perceive the promise of the younger artists of the nineteenth century. And it will be commended, as it deserves, for having kept alive through all the changes and developments of its policy a proper sense of artistic responsibility, and for having sought consistently to attach to itself as members those workers for whom distinction could not unreasonably be prophesied. How largely it succeeded in its aim will be proved, in the opinion of art historians, quite as much by the list of artists who made the society only a temporary stopping-place, as by the roll of members who lived and died in its ranks.

PLATES

PLATE I. "WAREHAM BRIDGE." BY H. G. HINE.

(By Permission of Messrs. Ernest Brown & Phillips.)

PLATE II. "THE STUDENT." BY CHAS. GREEN.

PLATE III.   "THE INFANT PAN."   BY GUIDO BACH.

PLATE IV. "A FRENCH FISHER GIRL." BY SIR J. D. LINTON.

PLATE V. "SOUTHWOLD FROM THE BEACH." BY TOM COLLIER.

(By Permission of Alexander M. Phillips, Esq.)

PLATE VI.   "THE BIRTHDAY."   BY E. J. GREGORY, R.A., P.R.I.

PLATE VII. "LINCOLN." BY JAMES ORROCK.

PLATE VIII. "SUSSEX." BY E. M. WIMPERIS.

PLATE IX. "MISFITS." BY SIR JOHN TENNIEL.

(By Permission of T. R. Way, Esq.)

PLATE X. "A DREARY STILLNESS SADDENING O'ER THE COAST." BY C. E. HOLLOWAY.

PLATE XI. "ON THE DOWNS NEAR HARTING." BY J. AUMONIER.

PLATE XII. "THE ROTUNDA AND CHAPEL OF THE HOLY SEPULCHRE." BY JOHN FULLEYLOVE.

(From "The Holy Land," published by Messrs. A. & C. Black.)

PLATE XIII. "APRIL." BY G. H. BOUGHTON, R.A.

PLATE XIV. "THE LAST FLIGHT." BY RANDOLPH CALDECOTT.

PLATE XV. "THE TOMBS OF THE KALIPHS, CAIRO." BY FRANK DILLON.

PLATE XVI. "MORNING MISTS, HEMINGFORD GREY." BY F. G. COTMAN.

PLATE XVII. LE FOLGOET. BY G. S. ELGOOD.

PLATE XVIII. "SALMON NETS, GAIRLOCH, ROSS-SHIRE." BY FRANK WALTON.

PLATE XIX. S. MARIA DELLA SALUTE. BY KEELEY HALSWELLE.

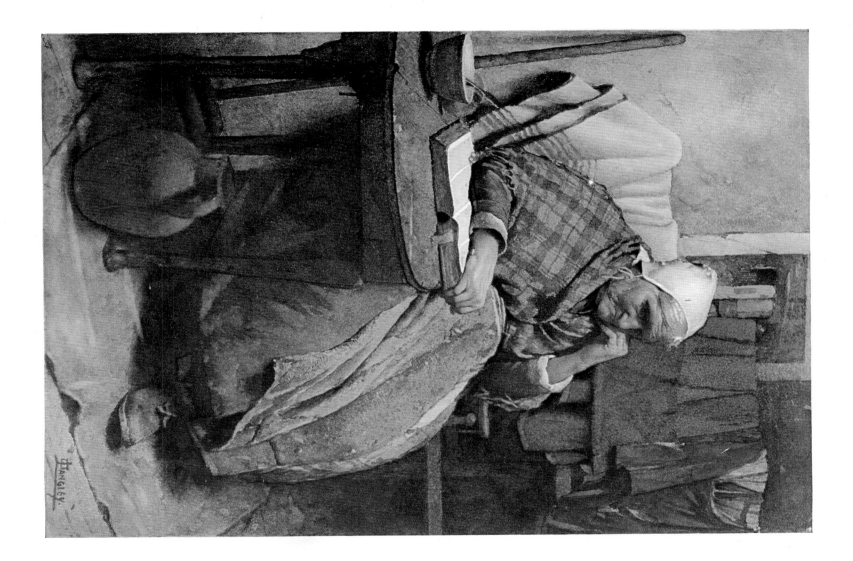

PLATE XX. "AN OLD CORNISH WOMAN." BY WALTER LANGLEY.

(By Permission of J. Henry Hill, Esq.)   PLATE XXI.   "A FISHERMAN'S TREASURE."   BY GEO. WETHERBEE.

PLATE XXII. "THOSE WHO SWIM IN SIN MUST SINK IN SORROW." BY FRANK DADD.

(By Permission of the President and Council of the Royal Institute.)

PLATE XXIII. "THE HAYFIELD." BY CLAUDE HAYES.

PLATE XXIV. "IN THE PARK." BY ALFRED EAST, A.R.A.

PLATE XXV. "THE IZAR AT TÖLZ." BY YEEND KING.

PLATE XXVI. "A HIGHLAND GLEN." BY A. W. WEEDON.

PLATE XXVII. "AN ALLEGORY." By JULES LESSORE.

PLATE XXVIII. "ON COME THE CURLED CLOUDS," BY BERNARD EVANS.

PLATE XXIX. "THE STREET SHOW." BY KATE GREENAWAY.

(By Permission of Frankland Gaskell, Esq.)　　　　　　　PLATE XXX. "A READER." BY ROBERT FOWLER.

PLATE XXXI. "THIS—ALL THIS WAS IN THE OLDEN TIME LONG AGO." BY ST. GEORGE HARE.

PLATE XXXII. "A WET DAY, OLD BERWICK BRIDGE." BY R. B. NISBET, R.S.A.

PLATE XXXIII. "THE LITTLE JACOB." BY HANS VON BARTELS.

PLATE XXXIV. "THE ART SCHOOL." BY JOHN P. GULICH.

PLATE XXXV. "PEONIES." BY DUDLEY HARDY.

PLATE xxxvi. "BE NEAR ME WHEN I FADE AWAY." BY W. LEE HANKEY.

PLATE XXXVII. "WHEN THE TIDE IS OUT." BY J. S. HILL.

PLATE XXXVIII. "SUNSET." BY G. C. HAITÉ.

PLATE XXXIX. "THE MERCHANT." By JOHN HASSALL.

PLATE XL. "SADNESS IN SPRING." BY JAMES CLARK.

NOW WHILE THE BIRDS THUS SING A JOYOUS SONG,
AND WHILE THE YOUNG LAMBS BOUND
AS TO THE TABOR'S SOUND,
TO ME ALONE THERE CAME A THOUGHT OF GRIEF:

WORDSWORTH

1416